HOW TO USE SOCIAL MEDIA FOR MARKETING

Beyond Trends: Crafting a Timeless Social Media Marketing Strategy.

LYNNE RUFFIN

Copyright © 2024 Lynne Ruffin.

All right reserved. No part of this book may be reproduced, stored in a retrieval system, or transmitted in any to or by any means, electronic, mechanical, photocopying, recording, scanning, or otherwise, without the prior written permission of the copyright owner.

Table of Content

Introduction

In the current digital era, social media has become an essential tool for businesses to interact with their target market, build brand awareness, and increase sales. With billions of active users across numerous platforms, social media offers businesses unparalleled opportunities to interact with customers, gather market insights, and promote products and services.

The Development of Social Media Marketing

Since Friendster and MySpace first launched, the concept of social media marketing has undergone significant transformation. In the past, social media was mostly used for networking and communication. However, when social media platforms like Facebook, Instagram, and Twitter gained popularity, businesses realized they could use them to accomplish their marketing goals.

Importance of Social Media Marketing

Social media marketing is essential to modern marketing campaigns for several reasons. Initially, it facilitates communication between businesses and a vast network of potential customers, especially those belonging to demographics that may be difficult to target with traditional marketing strategies. Social media also provides a means of increasing website traffic, fostering customer loyalty, and boosting brand exposure.

Understanding the Social Media Environment

To effectively leverage social media for marketing purposes, companies must understand the unique characteristics and target demographic of each platform. For example, Instagram is more popular with younger people and is better suited for visual content, whereas LinkedIn appeals to professionals and is great for B2B marketing.

The Power of Social Proof and Influencer Marketing

One of the key advantages of social media marketing is the utilization of influencer and social proof marketing. "Social proof" is a psychological phenomenon that explains how people are influenced by the opinions and actions of others. Companies can boost their credibility and reliability by showcasing user-generated content, endorsements from influencers, and customer reviews.

The process of advertising products and services by collaborating with individuals who have a substantial social media following is known as influencer marketing. Influencers can strengthen a business's relationship with its target audience and lend credibility to its advertising initiatives.

Social Media Marketing: Possibilities and Difficulties

Despite all of social media marketing's benefits, there are disadvantages for businesses. Managing their online reputation, replying to negative comments, and maintaining their authenticity are some of the biggest challenges that businesses face when using social media. Additionally, due to the rapid evolution of social media algorithms and features, businesses need to maintain flexibility and adjust their strategy as needed.

However, these challenges also present opportunities for businesses to differentiate themselves and outperform their competitors. By utilizing new features and trends, providing informative content, and communicating with customers in a genuine way, businesses may build meaningful relationships with their audience and achieve quantifiable results.

Considerations for Social Media Marketing Ethics

Ethical considerations are crucial in social media marketing since businesses must abide by the law, respect user privacy, and maintain transparency. As concerns about data privacy and internet security rise, businesses must prioritize ethical procedures if they hope to win over their audience's trust and credibility through social media marketing.

The Position of Social Media Marketing in the Digital Marketing Mix

Social media marketing is not the only component of a comprehensive digital marketing strategy. When used with email marketing, search engine optimization (SEO), and content marketing, social media may optimize marketing efforts and produce better results. By exploiting the connections between different platforms, businesses can create cohesive and effective marketing campaigns that resonate with their target market.

The Future of Social Media Marketing

Social media marketing has countless opportunities going forward as both technology and customer behavior develop further. It is anticipated that new technologies such as artificial intelligence (AI), virtual reality (VR), and augmented reality (AR) will change the social media marketing landscape. These technologies will present organizations with new opportunities for innovative audience communication.

Additionally, as social media platforms expand and include new features and activities, businesses must keep up with these developments and adapt their strategy. By embracing new trends and technology, businesses can stay ahead of the curve and leverage social media to generate significant returns on their marketing spending.

Social media marketing has become an essential component of modern marketing strategy since it gives businesses the greatest opportunity to interact with their target audience, build a solid brand, and increase sales. By understanding the unique characteristics and audience demographics of each platform, utilizing influencer marketing and social proof, and giving ethical issues first importance, businesses may effectively use social media to achieve their marketing objectives. With consumer behavior shifting and technology always evolving, social media marketing offers a bright future for businesses that can remain adaptable and creative in this fast-paced landscape.

Chapter One

Understanding Different Social Media Platforms

In today's digital environment, social media platforms are becoming essential tools for businesses looking to connect with their target audience, build brand awareness, and foster engagement. Businesses must recognize the subtle differences between the multiple platforms at their disposal, each aimed at a different set of users and demographics, in order to make the most of them as marketing tools.

Overview of Major Platforms

Facebook

Facebook is still one of the largest and most well-known social networking sites, with over 2.8 billion monthly active members worldwide. There are several options available, including personal profiles, company sites, groups, and events. Businesses can use Facebook to publish information, run targeted advertising campaigns, and interact with followers through comments and messages. Facebook's extensive targeting options and strong advertising platform make it an excellent tool for businesses looking to improve conversions and target certain demographics.

Instagram

Instagram is a picture-sharing and video-sharing social networking platform. With over 1 billion monthly active users, it gives businesses the opportunity to promote their products or services through visually appealing material. Instagram's features, such as Stories, Reels, and IGTV, give businesses innovative ways to interact with their audience and boost engagement. Instagram's shopping features allow businesses to tag things in their posts and stories, making it easier for consumers to search for and purchase goods directly from the platform.

Twitter

Twitter is a popular microblogging platform recognized for its concise content and instantaneous updates. Twitter has over 330 million active users each month and is a popular platform for people to share news, updates, and opinions on a variety of issues. Businesses can utilize Twitter to respond to customer direct messages and comments, provide timely updates, and join trending topics by utilizing hashtags. By using Twitter's advertising platform to promote tweets, profiles, and trends, businesses may increase engagement and reach a larger audience.

LinkedIn

LinkedIn is a professional networking service used by over 700 million individuals globally. Its main goals are job hunting, industry-related material, and professional networking. Businesses may network with new partners and clients on LinkedIn, establish thought leadership, and showcase their skills through postings and articles. Because LinkedIn's advertising platform lets businesses target employees based on job title, industry, and other criteria, it's a wonderful tool for lead generation and business-to-business (B2B) marketing.

Demographics and User Behavior

For businesses to modify their marketing strategy effectively, they need to be aware of the user behavior and demographics of each social media site. Below is a summary of user behavior and demographics on the major social media networks:

Facebook: Although it has a large user base, the majority of its users are in the 18–49 age range. People use the platform for 58 minutes a day on average, which is why both men and women find it appealing.

Instagram: Popular among younger demographics, Instagram's user base is primarily composed of individuals between the ages of 18 and 34. On average, users spend thirty minutes a day on the platform; users who are female and live in urban areas really enjoy it.

Twitter: Compared to other networks, Twitter has a relatively younger user base, with the majority of its members being between the ages of 18 and 29. The network is popular among urbanites and higher-educated people, with users spending an average of three minutes every day on it.

LinkedIn: Professionals and business professionals use LinkedIn primarily; the majority of its users are between the ages of 25 and 49. Users spend an average of 17 minutes per day on the platform; among its targeted demographics are those with higher levels of education and wealth.

By modifying their content, messaging, and advertising tactics in light of these user habits and demographics, businesses may effectively reach their intended audience on each platform.

Ultimately, understanding the unique characteristics of different platforms is essential for companies looking to leverage social media for marketing purposes. By changing their content, marketing, and advertising strategies based on an understanding of the capabilities, demographics, and user behavior of each platform, businesses can effectively engage with their target audience and accomplish results. Whether it's showing products on Instagram, reaching a big audience on Facebook, engaging in real-time conversations on Twitter, or networking with professionals on LinkedIn, each platform offers a unique opportunity for businesses to engage with their audience and achieve their marketing objectives.

Chapter Two

Setting SMART Goals for Social Media Marketing

One of the most important initial steps to success in the world of social media marketing is setting goals. However, not all goals are created equal. Establishing SMART goals—specific, measurable, achievable, relevant, and time-bound—is essential to ensuring the effectiveness and direction of your efforts in social media marketing. By following the SMART framework, businesses can establish specific goals that impact their social media strategy and ultimately yield significant rewards.

Specific Goals

Because specific goals are clearly stated and well-defined, there is no room for uncertainty. Setting specific goals is essential when creating objectives for your social media marketing. An example of a targeted goal would be, "increase brand awareness among millennials by 20% in the next six months," as opposed to a general goal of simply "increase brand awareness."

Measurable Goals

Measurable goals can be measured and allow for measuring progress over time. By establishing quantitative targets, businesses may evaluate whether they are getting closer to achieving their objectives. Metrics such as website traffic, engagement rate, follower growth, and conversion rate can be employed to evaluate the effectiveness of different strategies and measure the accomplishment of social media marketing campaigns.

Practical Goals

Realistic goals are reasonable and achievable given the organization's constraints and resources. When setting achievable goals for social media marketing, budget, personnel, and time constraints are all important factors to take into account. Overzealous ambition and setting objectives that are beyond the capabilities of the organization may result in dissatisfaction and disappointment. Instead, focus on creating goals that will push you but are still attainable.

Pertinent Goals

Relevant goals align with the overall objectives and top priorities of the company. It's critical to set social media marketing goals that align with larger business objectives, such as increasing sales, improving customer satisfaction, or launching a new product. Goals that are not directly related to the main business objectives may take resources and attention away from more important tasks.

Time-bound Goals

Time-bound goals have an end date or deadline by which they must be completed. Setting deadlines for tasks encourages a sense of urgency and facilitates effective work prioritization and resource allocation. Setting time-bound goals for social media marketing requires the development of precise deadlines and achievement markers. An objective that has a deadline, such "increase website traffic by 25% within the next three months," would be more specific than "increase website traffic."

An Example of SMART Social Media Marketing Goal-Setting

Let's examine an example of how a business may create goals for its social media marketing efforts using the SMART framework:

Details: To improve brand recognition, target millennials in the 18–34 age range with a focused Instagram advertising approach.

Achievable: Obtain a 5% engagement rate on campaign posts and gain 10% more Instagram followers in three months.

Achievable: Allocate $2,000 for the budget of the advertising campaign, and appoint a social media manager whose job it is to monitor and improve campaign results.

Important: Increasing brand recognition among millennials aligns with the company's objective of drawing in a younger demographic and expanding its customer base.

Transient: Start the Instagram marketing campaign by March 1st. Next, evaluate performance metrics each month to track your advancement toward your goals.

Setting SMART objectives for social media marketing is essential for directing strategies, evaluating advancement, and producing results. By setting goals that are Specific, Measurable, Achievable, Relevant, and Time-bound, businesses can ensure that their social media marketing activities are effective, focused, and aligned with larger corporate objectives. SMART goals provide a clear path to success in the dynamic and ever-evolving world of social media marketing by boosting website traffic, generating leads and conversions, and raising brand awareness.

Chapter Three

Creating a Social Media Strategy

In the present computerized age, a clear cut online entertainment procedure is fundamental for organizations hoping to use the force of virtual entertainment for the purpose of showcasing. An essential way to deal with web-based entertainment permits organizations to really draw in with their main interest group, fabricate brand mindfulness, drive site traffic, and eventually, accomplish their promoting goals. This article will investigate the vital parts of formulating an online entertainment technique, including distinguishing interest group, content preparation and creation, commitment methodologies, promoting, and planning.

Identifying Target Audience

The most important phase in thinking up an online entertainment methodology is distinguishing the interest group. Figuring out the socioeconomics, interests, ways of behaving, and inclinations of your interest group is critical for fitting your virtual entertainment content and messages to impact them. Directing statistical surveying, investigating client information, and utilizing crowd bits of knowledge devices given by web-based entertainment stages can assist organizations with acquiring a more profound comprehension of their interest group.

When the interest group has been recognized, organizations ought to make purchaser personas - fictitious portrayals of their optimal clients. Purchaser personas help organizations envision and comprehend their main interest group better, permitting them to fit their online entertainment content and messages to address the particular necessities, trouble spots, and inclinations of their ideal interest group sections.

Content Planning and Creation

Subsequent to distinguishing the interest group, the following stage is to foster a substance plan and make drawing in satisfied that impacts them. Content arranging includes deciding the kinds of content to make, the recurrence of posting, and the channels to convey content on. Organizations ought to consider making a substance schedule to coordinate and timetable their virtual entertainment content ahead of time.

While making content for web-based entertainment, it's fundamental for center around offering some benefit to the crowd. Whether it's instructive, engaging, uplifting, or useful, content ought to be applicable, legitimate, and locking in. Visual substance like pictures, recordings, and infographics will in general perform well via web-based entertainment and can assist organizations with catching the consideration of their crowd.

Not withstanding natural substance, organizations ought to likewise consider integrating client created content (UGC) into their web-based entertainment technique. UGC, for example, client surveys, tributes, and photographs shared by clients, can assist fabricate believability and entrust with the crowd.

Engagement Strategies

Commitment is a basic part of virtual entertainment showcasing, as it permits organizations to encourage significant associations with their crowd and construct connections after some time. Commitment techniques include associating with devotees, answering remarks and messages, and taking part in discussions via web-based entertainment. Organizations ought to effectively screen their web-based entertainment channels for notices, remarks, and messages and answer speedily and truly. Drawing in with devotees reinforces connections as well as refines the brand and fabricate entrust with the crowd.

Not withstanding responsive commitment, organizations ought to likewise integrate proactive commitment procedures into their virtual entertainment system. This might incorporate starting discussions with supporters, seeking clarification on pressing issues, running surveys or challenges, and empowering client produced content.

Advertising and Budgeting

While natural reach and commitment are significant, organizations ought to likewise consider integrating paid promoting into their virtual entertainment procedure to contact a more extensive crowd and drive explicit results. Online entertainment promoting permits organizations to target explicit socioeconomics, interests, and ways of behaving, guaranteeing that their messages contact the perfect crowd at the ideal time.

With regards to virtual entertainment promoting, it's fundamental for set clear goals and assign financial plan as needs be. Whether the objective is to increment brand mindfulness, drive site traffic, produce leads, or drive changes, organizations ought to designate spending plan in view of their goals and the normal profit from speculation (return for money invested).

Organizations can browse an assortment of promoting choices presented by online entertainment stages, including supported posts, show advertisements, video promotions, merry go round promotions, and the sky is the limit from there. It's essential to constantly screen and upgrade publicizing efforts to guarantee they are conveying the ideal outcomes and amplifying return for capital invested.

Thinking up an online entertainment procedure is fundamental for organizations hoping to use the force of virtual entertainment for the purpose of showcasing. By distinguishing the interest group, fostering a substance plan, carrying out commitment techniques, and consolidating paid publicizing, organizations can really draw in with their crowd, construct brand mindfulness, drive site traffic, and accomplish their promoting goals via online entertainment stages. With a distinct virtual entertainment methodology set up, organizations can tackle the maximum capacity of web-based entertainment to develop their image and drive business results.

Chapter Four

Optimizing Profiles and Content for Each Platform

In the domain of virtual entertainment advertising, enhancing profiles and content for every stage is fundamental for expanding reach, commitment, and eventually, driving outcomes. With every web-based entertainment stage having its own remarkable highlights, crowd socioeconomics, and content configurations, it's critical for organizations to tailor their profiles and content to resound with their main interest group on every stage really. This article will investigate the critical parts of enhancing profiles and content for web-based entertainment stages, including profile arrangement and marking, content rules, and best practices.

Profile Setup and Branding

The most vital phase in streamlining profiles for online entertainment showcasing is guaranteeing that profiles are set up accurately and mirror the brand character really. This incorporates picking a profile picture and cover photograph that line up with the brand's visual character and values. The profile picture ought to be a high-goal picture of the brand logo or a delegate picture that mirrors the brand's character, while the cover photograph gives an open door to exhibit the brand's items, administrations, or values.

Moreover, organizations ought to guarantee that their profile bio is compact, enlightening, and incorporates significant watchwords to further develop discoverability. The bio ought to give a concise outline of the brand, its items or administrations, and a source of inspiration (CTA) empowering clients to make a particular move, like visiting the site, pursuing a pamphlet, or reaching the business.

Consistency is key with regards to marking across online entertainment stages. Organizations ought to utilize steady marking components like tones, text styles, and informing across all online entertainment profiles to make a strong brand character and make it more straightforward for clients to perceive and recollect the brand.

Content Guidelines and Best Practices

Whenever profiles are set up and marked actually, the subsequent stage is to make and share content that resounds with the ideal interest group on every stage. Every web-based entertainment stage has its own substance rules and best practices that organizations ought with comply to while making and sharing substance.

Facebook: On Facebook, organizations ought to zero in on making outwardly captivating substance, for example, photographs, recordings, and merry go round posts. It's vital to utilize excellent pictures and recordings, incorporate subtitles or message overlays to pass on key messages, and consolidate a blend of special and educational substance to keep the crowd locked in.

Instagram: Instagram is a visual-driven stage, making it ideal for sharing great photographs and recordings. Organizations ought to zero in on making outwardly engaging substance that features their items or administrations in a real and imaginative manner. Instagram Stories and Reels are additionally famous organizations for sharing in the background content, item shows, and drawing in with adherents continuously.

Twitter: Twitter is known for its continuous updates and short-structure content. Organizations ought to zero in on sharing brief and connecting with tweets that catch the consideration of their crowd. Visual substance like pictures, GIFs, and recordings will generally perform well on Twitter and can assist organizations with hanging out in clients' channels.

LinkedIn: LinkedIn is an expert systems administration stage, making it ideal for sharing industry-related content, thought initiative articles, and profession related refreshes. Organizations ought to zero in on making educational and significant substance that teaches and moves their crowd. LinkedIn's distributing stage permits organizations to share long-structure articles and blog entries, situating them as industry specialists and naturally suspected pioneers.

As well as observing stage explicit substance rules, organizations ought to likewise consider best practices like posting reliably, captivating with supporters, utilizing applicable hashtags, and breaking down execution measurements to enhance content system over the long haul.

Advancing profiles and content for every web-based entertainment stage is fundamental for boosting reach, commitment, and eventually, driving outcomes in virtual entertainment promoting. By guaranteeing that profiles are set up and marked really, and by observing substance rules and best practices for every stage, organizations can make a firm and drawing in web-based entertainment presence that resounds with their interest group and accomplishes their promoting targets. With an essential way to deal with improving profiles and content, organizations can use the force of virtual entertainment to fabricate brand mindfulness, drive site traffic, and at last, develop their business.

Chapter Five

Building and Growing a Following

Building and growing a following through web-based diversion is crucial for associations wanting to utilize the power of these stages for advancing. A strong and attracted following helps increase with stamping care and reach as well as gives associations a steady group that can drive site traffic, produce leads, and in the end, add to business improvement. This article will research the imperative philosophies for building and growing a following through virtual diversion, including normal improvement frameworks, paid headway methods, and stalwart associations.

Organic Growth Strategies

Regular improvement techniques base on attracting fans and growing responsibility through non-paid procedures. While regular improvement could carve out opportunity to achieve stood out from paid headway, it can achieve a more attracted and loyal following for a really long time. The following are a characteristic improvement philosophies associations can complete to create and foster their following by means of online diversion:

1. *Consistent Posting:* Consistency is key with respect to regular improvement through online amusement. Associations should spread out a conventional introducing plan and stick on it to

keep their group associated with and interested.

2. ***High-Quality Content:*** Making predominant grade, huge substance is crucial for attracting and holding followers. Associations should focus in on making content that is helpful, connecting with, and appropriate to their primary vested party.

3. ***Engagement with Followers:*** Successfully enthralling with fans by noting comments, messages, and notification can help with building associations and energize a sensation of neighborhood virtual diversion.

4. ***Hashtag Strategy:*** Using significant hashtags in posts can grow detectable quality and show up at through web-based amusement stages. Associations should explore

and use hashtags that are appropriate to their industry, principal vested party, and content.

5. *Collaborations and Cross-Promotion:* Cooperating with various associations, forces to be reckoned with, or content creators in a comparable specialty can help with reaching a greater group and attract new lovers. Cross-propelling substance with complementary brands can similarly help with extending transparency and responsibility.

Paid Promotion Techniques

Paid progression methods incorporate taking care of money to contact a greater group and accelerate enthusiast improvement through internet based diversion stages. While paid progression requires a money related adventure, it will in general be an effective strategy for growing detectable quality, reach, and responsibility. Here are some paid progression systems associations can use to foster their following by means of online amusement:

1. *Social Media Advertising:* Virtual diversion publicizing licenses associations to propel their substance, things, or organizations to an assigned group on stages like Facebook, Instagram, Twitter, and LinkedIn. Associations can make assigned advancement campaigns considering economics, interests, approaches to acting, and more to show up at anticipated lovers and drive responsibility.

2. ***Promoted Posts:*** Propelling posts by means of electronic diversion stages can help with growing detectable quality and reach among a greater group. Associations can help their top-performing presents on show up at extra clients and attract new fans.

3. ***Sponsored Content:*** Collaborating with forces to be reckoned with or content producers to create upheld content can help associations with showing up at their ideal vested party and attract new fans. Upheld content can show up as upheld posts, upheld stories, upheld accounts, from that point, anything is possible.

4. ***Social Media Difficulties and Giveaways:*** Working with difficulties and giveaways through online

amusement stages can help associations with extending responsibility, attract new enthusiasts, and become their following. Associations can encourage clients to partake in difficulties by adoring, commenting, sharing, or naming friends.

Influencer Partnerships

Stalwart associations incorporate cooperating with powerhouses or content creators who influence online amusement stages. Working together with forces to be reckoned with can help associations with reaching an assigned group, increase brand care, and attract new allies. The following are a couple of philosophies for building and growing a thoroughly completing stalwart associations:

1. ***Identify Appropriate Influencers:*** Associations should recognize forces to be reckoned with who line up with their picture values, ideal vested party, and advancing targets. Exploring forces to be reckoned with's substance, responsibility, and group economics can help with perceiving the right powerhouses for affiliations.

2. ***Collaborate on Upheld Content:*** Collaborating with forces to be reckoned with to create upheld content can help associations with reaching a greater group and attract new enthusiasts. Upheld content can show up as upheld posts, upheld stories, upheld accounts, and that is just a glimpse of something larger.

3. ***Run Force to be reckoned with Takeovers:*** Allowing forces to be reckoned with to take command over a brand's electronic diversion address a day or a specific event can help with extending responsibility, attract new fans, and give another perspective on the brand.,

4. ***Offer Partner Partnerships:*** Offering branch-off associations to rockin' rollers can help them to propel the brand and drive fan advancement. Associations can give forces to be reckoned with extraordinary discount codes or part interfaces with follow changes and reimburse powerhouses considering execution.

Building and growing a following by means of virtual diversion requires a fundamental technique that joins normal improvement systems, paid headway methodologies, and stalwart associations. Via doing a mix of these systems, associations can attract and hold allies, increase responsibility, and finally, drive business improvement through virtual diversion advancing. Whether it's making great substance, placing assets into virtual diversion advancing, or collaborating with forces to be reckoned with, building and growing a following through internet based diversion requires resistance, consistency, and a significant perception of the vested party and stage components. With a reasonable method for managing enthusiast improvement, associations can utilize the power of virtual diversion to achieve their exhibiting objectives and prosper in the present electronic scene.

Chapter Six

Analyzing and Measuring Performance

Dissecting and estimating execution is a basic part of web-based entertainment showcasing, as it permits organizations to assess the viability of their procedures, track progress towards objectives, and go with information driven choices to enhance their promoting endeavors. By checking key measurements and utilizing examination instruments, organizations can acquire important bits of knowledge into their web-based entertainment execution, distinguish regions for development, and change their techniques in like manner. This article will investigate the significance of examining and estimating execution in online entertainment advertising, key measurements to follow, and the job of examination devices in driving achievement.

Key Metrics and Analytics Tools

Examining and estimating execution in online entertainment promoting is fundamental because of multiple factors:

1. *Evaluation of Effectiveness:* By dissecting execution measurements, organizations can decide if their virtual entertainment advertising endeavors are accomplishing the ideal outcomes and meeting their targets. This permits organizations to recognize areas of accomplishment and

regions for development in their systems.

2. *Identification of Patterns and Patterns:* Breaking down execution information can assist organizations with recognizing patterns and examples in crowd conduct, content execution, and commitment measurements. This understanding can illuminate future substance procedure and assist organizations with remaining in front of patterns in the steadily developing scene of web-based entertainment.

3. *Optimization of Strategies:* By following execution measurements and examining information, organizations can distinguish regions where their methodologies can be upgraded for improved

results. This might include changing substance technique, focusing on rules, promotion spend allotment, or commitment strategies in light of experiences gathered from execution information.

4. *Demonstration of ROI:* Dissecting execution measurements permits organizations to exhibit the profit from speculation (return on initial capital investment) of their virtual entertainment promoting endeavors. By evaluating the effect of web-based entertainment on key business goals, for example, brand mindfulness, site traffic, lead age, and deals, organizations can legitimize their interest in virtual entertainment showcasing.

Adjusting Strategies Based on Data

With regards to examining and estimating execution in virtual entertainment advertising, there are a few key measurements that organizations ought to track to assess the viability of their systems. These measurements can be comprehensively ordered into three primary regions: crowd commitment, content execution, and business influence. Here are a vital measurements to follow in every classification:

Crowd Engagement:

Devotee Growth: The rate at which the crowd is developing over the long run.

Commitment Rate: The level of adherents who draw in with your substance through likes, remarks, offers, and snaps.

Reach and Impressions: The quantity of clients who have seen your substance (reach) and the complete number of times your substance has been seen (impressions).

Content Performance:

Post Performance: The presentation of individual posts concerning likes, remarks, shares, and other commitment measurements.

Content Reach: The scope of individual bits of content and how it looks at to other substance.

Content Type: The exhibition of various sorts of content (e.g., pictures, recordings, joins) with regards to commitment and reach.

Business Impact:

Site Traffic: how much traffic headed to your site from virtual entertainment stages.

Lead Generation: The quantity of leads produced through virtual entertainment channels.

Transformation Rate: The level of virtual entertainment clients who make an ideal move (e.g., making a buy, pursuing a pamphlet).

Profit from Speculation (ROI): The proportion of the return produced from web-based entertainment showcasing endeavors to the venture put forth in those attempts.

Examination Instruments for Estimating Execution

There are various examination devices accessible to help organizations measure and break down execution in online entertainment promoting. These apparatuses give significant bits of knowledge into crowd conduct, content execution, and the effect of web-based entertainment on business goals. Here are some well known examination devices for estimating execution in virtual entertainment advertising:

Facebook Insights: Facebook Experiences gives itemized investigation on crowd socioeconomics, post execution, reach, commitment, and something else for Facebook Pages.

Instagram Insights: Instagram Experiences offers investigation on crowd socioeconomics, content execution, impressions, reach, and commitment for Instagram Business accounts.

Twitter Analytics: Twitter Investigation gives experiences into crowd socioeconomics, tweet execution, impressions, commitment, and devotee development for Twitter accounts.

LinkedIn Analytics: LinkedIn Investigation offers information on crowd socioeconomics, post execution, impressions, commitment, and adherent development for LinkedIn Pages.

Google Analytics: Google Examination can be utilized to follow site traffic and transformations driven by virtual entertainment channels, giving experiences into the effect of web-based entertainment on site execution and business objectives.

Outsider Investigation Tools: There are likewise various outsider examination apparatuses accessible that give complete experiences and examination to different web-based entertainment stages, like Fledgling Social, Hootsuite, Cushion, and Socialbakers.

Changing Methodologies In light of Information

Whenever organizations have investigated execution measurements and acquired bits of knowledge from examination apparatuses, the following stage is to change their web-based entertainment procedures in view of the information. Here are a few systems for changing virtual entertainment procedures in light of execution information:

1. *Content Optimization:* Use bits of knowledge from content execution measurements to enhance content methodology by zeroing in on satisfied sorts and points that resound most with the crowd.

2. *Audience Targeting:* Use experiences from crowd commitment measurements to refine crowd

focusing on standards and contact the most applicable crowd portions with web-based entertainment content.

3. ***Ad Spend Allocation:*** Use experiences from paid advancement measurements to change promotion spend allotment and streamline advertisement lobbies for better execution and return for capital invested.

4. ***Engagement Tactics:*** Use bits of knowledge from commitment measurements to refine commitment strategies and procedures, like timing of posts, recurrence of posting, and kinds of commitment exercises.

5. ***Goal Setting:*** Use bits of knowledge from business influence measurements to define new

objectives and goals for virtual entertainment advertising endeavors in view of execution information and business targets.

By persistently dissecting execution measurements and changing web-based entertainment procedures in light of information driven experiences, organizations can enhance their virtual entertainment showcasing endeavors for improved results and drive outcome in accomplishing their advertising goals.

Breaking down and estimating execution is a pivotal part of web-based entertainment showcasing that permits organizations to assess the viability of their systems, track progress towards objectives, and go with information driven choices to upgrade their promoting endeavors. By checking key measurements, utilizing examination devices, and changing systems in light of execution information, organizations can acquire important experiences into their web-based entertainment execution, recognize regions for development, and drive outcome in accomplishing their promoting targets. With an essential way to deal with investigating and estimating execution, organizations can outfit the force of online entertainment to construct brand mindfulness, drive site traffic, produce leads, and at last, accomplish their promoting objectives.

Chapter Seven

Staying Up-to-Date with Trends and Changes

In the dynamic and continuously propelling scene of virtual amusement advancing, keeping alert to-date with examples and changes is principal for associations expecting to involve the greatest limit of these stages for the ultimate objective of exhibiting. From estimation updates to emerging stages and features, remaining informed concerning the latest examples and changes grants associations to change their frameworks, attract with their group effectively, and stay before the resistance. This article will research the meaning of keeping alert to-date with examples and changes in virtual diversion publicizing, the impact of electronic amusement computation revives, and emerging stages and features shaping the possible destiny of online diversion exhibiting.

Meaning of Keeping alert to-Date with Examples and Changes

Keeping alert to-date with examples and changes in online diversion exhibiting is basic in light of various variables:

1. *Adaptability:* The online diversion scene is ceaselessly creating, with new stages, components, and examples emerging reliably. Keeping alert to-date allows associations to change their frameworks and techniques to utilize new entryways and stay before the resistance.

2. *Relevance:* Electronic amusement stages are persistently invigorating their computations and familiarizing new features with further foster client experience and responsibility. Keeping alert to-date with these movements ensures that associations can make content that resonates with their group and stays huge in the continuously evolving online diversion scene.

3. *Effectiveness:* By keeping alert to-date with examples and changes, associations can further develop their electronic diversion advancing undertakings for further developed results. Whether it's using new features to augment responsibility or changing substance system considering estimation revives, staying informed grants

associations to support the sufficiency of their online diversion advancing undertakings.

4. *Competitive Advantage:* In the serious universe of online diversion exhibiting, keeping alert to-date with examples and changes can give associations a high ground. By being out before the resistance, associations can get the thought of their group, hang out in stuffed deals with, and separate themselves from competitors.

Social Media Algorithm Updates

Virtual diversion estimations expect a basic part in concluding the substance that clients see on their feeds. Understanding how these computations work and keeping alert to-date with estimation revives is crucial for associations expecting to extend their compass and responsibility by means of online amusement stages. The following are a couple of key examinations concerning on the web diversion computation invigorates:

1. **Content Relevance:** Online amusement estimations center around glad that is huge and associating with to clients. This consolidates content that earns raised college educations of responsibility like inclinations, comments, offers, and snaps.

2. **User Engagement:** Computations consider client responsibility signals like inclinations, comments, offers, and time spent on fulfilled to choose its importance and spotlight on it in clients' feeds.

3. **Content Format:** Estimations could lean toward explicit substance setups like accounts, pictures, or live streams considering client tendencies and responsibility plans.

4. **Frequency of Posting:** Estimations could rebuff accounts that post a lot of the time or too conflictingly, influencing their compass and detectable quality on the stage.

5. **Quality of Content:** Estimations center around perfect, dependable substance that offers an advantage to clients and works on their experience on the stage.

Observing estimation updates and understanding what they mean for content detectable quality and responsibility is major for associations wanting to upgrade their virtual amusement advancing undertakings and extend their reach and responsibility through electronic diversion stages.

Emerging Platforms and Features

Despite computation revives, keeping alert to-date with emerging stages and features is major for associations expecting to stay in control in online amusement exhibiting. Emerging stages and features offer new entryways for associations to communicate with their group, attempt various things with new fulfilled organizes, and separate themselves from competitors. The following are a couple emerging stages and features framing the destiny of virtual diversion exhibiting:

1. **TikTok:** TikTok has in the blink of an eye climbed to prominence as potentially of the fastest creating

social medium stages, particularly among more energetic economics. With its short-structure video setup and complement on creative mind and validness, TikTok offers associations an important opportunity to contact a more young group and make attracting blissful in a significantly savvy environment.

2. **Instagram Reels:** Instagram Reels is a short-structure video incorporate that licenses clients to make and share 15-second accounts set up with a decent soundtrack. Like TikTok, Reels offers associations an entryway to show off their things or organizations in a creative and interfacing way, contact a greater group, and augmentation brand detectable quality on Instagram.

3. **Live Streaming:** Live streaming has become dynamically popular by means of online amusement stages, with stages like Facebook, Instagram, and YouTube offering live electronic features. Live streaming licenses associations to attract with their group persistently, have virtual events, thing dispatches, ever changing conversations, and behind the scenes content, empowering a sensation of validity and relationship with their group.

4. **Social Commerce:** Social business is an emerging example that organizes web business incorporates directly into online amusement stages, allowing clients to find, scrutinize, and purchase things without leaving the stage. Features like Instagram

Shopping, Facebook Shops, and Pinterest Shop license associations to show off their things and drive bargains directly through electronic diversion.w

5. **Augmented Reality (AR) and PC created Reality (VR):** Extended reality (AR) and increased reality (VR) developments are ending up being dynamically planned into electronic diversion stages, offering associations new opportunities to make clear and clever experiences for their group. Features, for instance, AR channels, central focuses, and virtual have a go at experiences license associations to attract with their group in imaginative ways and drive brand responsibility.

Keeping alert to-date with examples and changes in virtual amusement advancing is central for associations wanting to involve the most extreme limit of these stages for publicizing. From staying informed about electronic amusement computation updates to researching emerging stages and features, staying ready licenses associations to change their

Chapter Eight

Case Studies and Examples of Successful Social Media Campaigns

Electronic amusement has transformed into a necessary resource for promoters to connect with their group, manufacture brand care, and drive responsibility. Through inventive and key missions, associations have had the choice to utilize the reach and effect of electronic amusement stages to achieve their promoting targets and drive significant results. In this article, we'll examine context oriented examinations and examples of productive electronic diversion campaigns that have made a colossal difference and set new rules for strong advancing methods.

1. Airbnb's LiveThere Mission

Airbnb, the overall electronic business place for lodging and convenience organizations, shipped off the #LiveThere hall to ask pilgrims to experience protests like nearby individuals rather than tourists. The mission focused in on making real and striking travel experiences and was shipped off across various electronic amusement stages including Instagram, Twitter, and Facebook.

Key parts of the mission included client created content showing exceptional Airbnb postings and experiences, stalwart relationship with development bloggers and content producers, and attracting describing through accounts and photos.

The mission really exploited the yearning for veritable travel experiences and made limitless buzz and responsibility by means of virtual amusement.

2. Coca-Cola's "Offer a Coke"

Mission Coca-Cola's "Offer a Coke" campaign is an excellent delineation of how a redid and keen virtual diversion mission can drive responsibility and brand dependability. The mission remembered superseding the Coca-Cola logo for containers and containers with notable names, engaging customers to find and grant holders to their names or the names of friends and family.

The mission was shipped off across various electronic diversion stages with the hashtag #ShareACoke, enabling clients to share photos and records of their redid Coca-Cola bottles. The mission made gigantic client delivered content, extended brand responsibility, and invigorated buyer relationship with the Coca-Cola brand.

3. Nike's JustDoIt Mission with Colin Kaepernick

Nike's JustDoIt campaign including past NFL quarterback Colin Kaepernick began unfathomable conversation and conversation through web-based diversion. The mission, which featured Kaepernick with the caption "Confidence in something. Whether or not it suggests relinquishing everything," settled social and strategy driven issues associated with racial despicableness and police furiousness.

Notwithstanding facing response from specific buyers, the mission resounded with Nike's ideal vested party and got vast assistance and recognition by means of virtual amusement. The mission created basic brand care, supported Nike's picture lifestyle as a socially perceptive and moderate association, and drove a flood in arrangements and stock expenses.

4. Wendy's NuggsForCarter Mission

Wendy's, the modest pecking order known for its sassy and senseless virtual diversion presence, shipped off the NuggsForCarter entryway considering a tweet from a high schooler named Carter Wilkerson. Wilkerson tweeted at Wendy's requesting the number from retweets he would need to get free chicken fingers for a year, to which Wendy's replied with the trial of 18 million retweets.

The tweet turned into a web sensation, lighting a virtual diversion frenzy with clients empowering behind Wilkerson's main goal with the assumption for free lumps. Disregarding not showing up at the forceful goal of 18 million retweets, Wilkerson's tweet transformed into the most retweeted tweet ever, delivering colossal brand transparency and responsibility for Wendy's.

5. Old Zing's "The Man Your Man Could Smell Like"

Mission Old Zing's "The Man Your Man Could Smell Like" campaign is an extraordinary portrayal of how humor and imagination can drive brand care and responsibility through electronic diversion. The mission incorporated a movement of silly fittings and accounts highlighting performer Isaiah Mustafa, who portrayed a smooth and certain individual conveying shrewd and significant lines.

The mission was shipped off across various virtual diversion organizes and transformed into a web sensation, delivering a colossal number of points of view and offers. Old Flavor successfully rebranded itself as a front line and tense brand, attracting a more energetic fragment and reviving its image through shrewd and drawing in electronic diversion content.

Key Accomplishment Factors and Significant focuses

These context oriented examinations highlight a couple of key accomplishment components and center focuses for making successful virtual diversion campaigns:

1. **Authenticity and Relevance:** Productive missions resonate with

their ideal vested party by conveying true blue and material substance that lines up with their tendencies, values, and objectives.

2. **Engagement and Interaction:** Attracting with customers and engaging collaboration through client delivered content, difficulties, and troubles can drive brand responsibility and endurance.

3. **Innovation and Creativity:** Innovative and inventive missions that state of the art the chaos and catch thought can deliver buzz and virality through web-based amusement.

4. **Storytelling and Up close and personal Appeal:** Persuading describing and significant charm might solid areas for make with

purchasers and drive at any point brand affection and dedication.

5. **Adaptability and Flexibility:** Online diversion missions should be adaptable and versatile to answer changes in purchaser lead, stage estimations, and market designs.

These logical examinations and models show the power of online amusement promoting in driving brand care, responsibility, and business results. By using creative systems, attracting describing, and inventive substance, associations can make significant and critical electronic diversion campaigns that resonate with their group and drive significant results. With the right philosophy and execution, virtual amusement promoting might potentially lift brands, streak conversations, and make getting through relationship with buyers in the present old age.

Conclusion

With everything taken into account, online amusement has changed how associations partner with their group, build brand care, and drive responsibility. From making persuading substance to using imaginative frameworks, online diversion offers tremendous entryways for associations to reach and attract with their vested party in critical ways. All through this associate, we've researched various pieces of including online diversion for advancing, including spreading out goals, making techniques, making content, taking apart execution, and keeping alert to-date with examples and changes.

As associations continue to investigate the consistently creating scene of electronic diversion exhibiting, recalling two or three key guidelines is major:

1. *Audience-Driven Approach:* Productive web-based diversion advancing beginnings with a significant perception of the ideal vested party. By recognizing their tendencies, interests, and approaches to acting, associations can tailor their substance and messages to resonate with their group and drive responsibility.

2. *Consistency and Authenticity:* Consistency is key concerning virtual diversion promoting. Keeping a solid posting plan, brand voice, and visual person helps work with checking affirmation and endow with the group. Moreover, validness is indispensable for partnering with clients by means of

electronic amusement. Dependable substance that reflects the brand's characteristics and character will undoubtedly resound with the group and drive responsibility.

3. ***Data-Driven Decision Making:*** Exploring execution estimations and using assessment instruments is basic for progressing virtual amusement exhibiting tries. By following key estimations, associations can secure critical encounters into their group's approach to acting, content execution, and the impact of their displaying attempts, allowing them to make data driven decisions to additionally foster outcomes.

4. ***Adaptability and Innovation:*** The virtual diversion scene is persistently progressing, with new

stages, components, and examples emerging reliably. Associations ought to keep alert to-date with these movements and change their methods and systems to utilize new entryways and stay before the resistance. Besides, progression is key for hanging out in the pressed web-based diversion space. Investigating various roads in regards to new blissful courses of action, responsibility techniques, and creative contemplations can help associations with getting the thoughts of their group and drive results.

Pushing ahead, associations should focus on refining their virtual diversion techniques, investigating various roads in regards to new methodologies, and constantly looking at execution to drive result in their displaying tries. Whether it's making persuasive substance, attracting the group, or separating execution estimations, the way to result in web-based diversion advancing lies in getting a handle on the group, conveying regard, and staying composed in light of changes in the mechanized scene.

With everything taken into account, online diversion displaying offers associations a solid stage to connect with their group, build brand care, and drive business results. By using the norms and procedures shown in this helper, associations can open the most extreme limit of online diversion to achieve their advancing objectives and thrive in the present age.

www.ingramcontent.com/pod-product-compliance
Lightning Source LLC
Chambersburg PA
CBHW050042260726
48658CB00005B/1725